LITANY

of the

PLANTS

J. DAN PAQUETTE

outskirtspress
DENVER, COLORADO

Outskirts Press, Inc.
http://www.outskirtspress.com

ISBN: 978-1-4787-6086-3

Outskirts Press and the "OP" logo are trademarks belonging to Outskirts Press, Inc.

PRINTED IN THE UNITED STATES OF AMERICA

Contents

Acknowledgments

The author wishes to thank the editors of the publications where these poems originally appeared:

Along the Way; Poems of the Seattle Metaphorical Society: "Allegro," "Entry for November 27th, 2008," "Longmire Meadows," "Wooden Virtues"

Between the Lines: "Best Organism Contest"

Clamor: "Side by Side", "What Counts"

Douglasia: "Missing"

Lab Lit: "Your Task List for a Limestone Outcrop at a Road Cut East of Emporia on Old Highway 50"

Marshnotes: "The Sanctuary"

Native Plant Press (WNPS): "Landscapes on Opening Night," "Henry Satulick"

Switchback: "Polemic in Fragments"

A special thanks to my instructors, including Michael Hickey, J. Baugher, and David Wagoner. Thanks to fellow poets and scientists for their inspiration. I am also grateful for regular access to the library collections and databases at the University of Washington and the U.W. Herbarium. A special thanks to the editors and scientists assisting me with Latin case endings for botanical families, including Tom Blockheel, Phillip Oswald, and Benito Tan. Thanks also to Marcia Casey, Richard Dawkins, Christine Deavel, J.W. Marshall, the late Herb Pius and the late Albert White Hat Sr.—requiescant in pace.

FINISHING

4TH,

5TH

OR

LATER

Arrival
for T. Kano and E. Vineberg

A young female bonobo leaves home, leaves
an older brother with her mother, leaves
her tribe, joins another.
How's this done—when
she comes upon foraging strangers, no one
to make introductions.
Is there some secret sign,
maybe a big step forward, offering to groom an elder,
maybe an invitation from another female to engage
in genito-genital rubbing, or perhaps playing tag
with some youngsters?
She comes (as did her foremothers)
upon foraging strangers.
How is it done?

Raking Under the Big Leaf Maple
for Dick Decker

Stiff leaves dehisce. My wish
is to witness the slow renting
of cells, the leaf weaned
from the wood, the scar,

the soar and what follows—
leaves fleeing to earth
the patting of the grass
the brittle scratch on the walk.

Spent cells in the leaf lobes bent
as ballerina feet. Pulsing wind arrives
and just because they are able, leaves
embark once again, this time down the street.

Leaf tips scratching the asphalt
like ancient hands locked
in a pianist's first position, fleeing
from the hollowed tree trunk.

The tiered bark remains at home,
combed in columns.

Wooden Virtues

A late afternoon sun bathes the 10,000 needles
branched on a single six-inch hemlock stem.
Soon, this tree and its siblings will blacken
an already dark understory on this forest land.

Tomorrow, due to Earth's minute wobble,
the sun's different angle, a different hemlock
six feet away will bask in late coral ray,
end-of-day photosynthesis—an unexpected treat

like peach ice cream.

Cabinet posts are undertaken,
we have been told, by people
making great sacrifices
to work in the public sector.

Entry for November 27th, 2008

Your knees press unto the hemlock log
opposite me. Tush-to-heels, your nose
floats above a green moss coat clinging
to rutted rust-brown bark. A half-dome,
your back curled, a praying khaki'd burl.

On all sides, the frond ladders of ferns
stiffen, they no longer sway, but flame
against the sun's morning rays, leaflets
long exhausted from expelling a storm
of spores upon aphids gathered beneath.

Bushtits lighter than walnuts ravage
vine maple limbs in the ravine
below us, bobbing for leaf hoppers,
mites. This silent, needful violence
flits, bobbles along lean branches.

Closer, over your shoulder, the torso
of an alder. Its thin bark is whitened,
speckled in dots, flesh tone craters—
lichen pregnancy wards, perhaps fifty
in an area the size of a jelly jar cover.

Steam rises from our cups, condenses
on boughs of the red cedar above us,
its fronds photosynthesizing, exhaling
oxygen, and as water likewise escapes,
roots tug more moisture from beneath us.

Hiker stops. "Anything down this trail?"
Surrounding him on the soil's horizon
a dozen fungal species tunnel in a microscopic
meander, their branching noodles absorbing,
decomposing pine needles that have fallen.

Walking out of the woods, you engage
the Vega's hatch. We throw the wet packs
in above the green sign, the bumper sticker
framed in rose-colored concertina wire
announcing, *Every Day Is Memorial Day*.

It's also Thanksgiving and in town, we
stop at the county soup kitchen. Later,
we exult; we link elbows, we sashay,
move our molecules. We glide among neighbors
through several rounds of a Virginia Reel.

Saints Peter and Paul

do not appear in this here poem.

I would agree that they walk not
among organisms we regularly see.

In the endings of my beginnings,
if the third sperm from the left
had reached the egg first,

how different would she or he
have been from me?

Best Organism Contest

After the winner was announced,
the judges left by a midnight train.
Humans slammed the lids on their laptops;
those working in fields, kicking the dust;
students in coffee shops were texting
their mothers, as if they were apologizing
for a fluke at the World Cup.

12

In This Aisle:

Pork Button Bone
Pork Butt Chunk
Jowl Meat
Pork Butt Cubed for Stew

Pheasant
Whole Duck
Jumbo Quail
Young Kung Fu Turkey

Dried Pollack
Fresh Trout, Gutted
Frozen Flounder
Half-Dried Pollack

North American Adolescent
Young Adult Arm Roast
Organ Medley
Charles Roast

Quite Fond of Corduroy

My rancher dotes on those well-assembled,
yet troublesome trousers, and what came *before:*

he notes their maker—subdued seamstress, crumpled
in some wicked place, tacking, the table, the cloth;

and what comes *after:* for lack of clean laundry, he once more
slips into his cords. Midmorning, he's mending fence,

the fabric grinding away—tectonic plates stuck
in the groin's subducted, pliable rock.

His pants rend upon the top barbed wire. Human,
not geological noises voice an exclamation,

the inconvenience now visiting him, a pinch of martyrdom,
disappointment over the pants' life cycle, vexing him.

Side by Side

I'm tilling the soil so as to include
rows of potatoes, broccoli and kale.

I'm puffing. My lungs rasp, louder
than the piercing of this stony soil,
scraping out the dandelion stubble,
Canadian thistle. Soil's blackening.
Above, the puffs of charcoal clouds,
airborne potatoes, hubbard squash.

Pitchfork strains to fold the bottom
of my foot, the ground meanwhile,
floats a familiar fungal odor. Woe,
despondency of this day evaporate
in stillness, a nothingness of dusk,
my boot heel-to-toe, step onto fork.

Son shouts *supper* from the porch.
Comforting his preparation, soup's
now ladled, peppered, buttery fish
steaming, hot noodles sesame. For
what we are, and about to receive,
what will soon rise from the earth.

What Counts

I'm tilling the soil so as to include
rows of potatoes, broccoli and kale.

Each pitch of the fork churns forth
about five hundred billion bacteria,
five hundred million protozoa. Just
a slug or two, but as for nematodes,
around eighty thousand, springtails
and mites in the hundreds, pollen...

Mashing the dirt, such disturbance,
the majority, inconveniently jerked
skyward, turned upside down. But
of the unfortunates, perhaps one in
every thousand: stress, deficiencies,
one hundred fifty million fatalities.

Spores aborting, exposure, millions
of bacteria not living to next fission.
Still churning the plot (my plot and
theirs), controlling destinies, means
of reproduction. So add composting,
less tilling— for all of us, salvation?

Allegro

Follow
  me
    down
      this
        rock-torn
          trail
     past the snowy tops of grimmia moss
  past marmot nests and dark-eyed juncos,
     boughs of cedar, islands of willow,
        mountain alder and monkey flower.
        Then
       down
      this
   gentle
 slope
    past sunlit daisies and carex sedges
      flowering currant and rippling salmon streams;
    follow the ravens gliding on valley currents.
       Then into
         the
          silent forest
       past nursing logs and their hemlock children,
    beetles rambling over large leafy moss,
       past the fuzz balls of avens and bacterial blobs,
    past bitter cherry and bleeding heart,
      tree bark attired in turquoise lichens.

Follow me, lest
obsolete progress draws you again to the maze
of enslaved engineers, and wireless entrepreneurs,
their portfolios prefaced on animal carnage.
Follow me, for
maximum return on investment imposes
the squeezing, the bleeding of all species unnoticed.
Your family obligations, your mother's expectations:

Leave them all, and rescue this path from understated death
at the hands of long-distance humans.
Deliver us from their evil, Amen.

Sensory Meditation, Shoreview Park, 3:00 AM

I'm a federal government bureaucrat,
I ponder microeconomics while swallowing pills
and top-down pronouncements. My whining
ends when I arrive here at night, and sit

against a cedar's combed bark, legs dangling
over the ledge of the canyon, the moon
patches the night into silver and black.
I spread my knees: Below,

near the stream, a raccoon rests on a sandbar.
I inch on my jacket. Half-submerged stones
swallow my sounds. The raccoon immerses two paws,
the canyon, my cramping leg, my brain wait

to be stretched, the raccoon
struggles—like us, like everything else.
The struggle for existence—words dangling, separated
from the mixing bowl of Judeo-Christian tradition.

Some economic shit stands on its own,
the raccoon corrals something, a crawfish?
What would change in a world that was not adverse
to the interests of raccoons, of crawfish,

of all living things? We accept the national interest,
interest of unliving things like corporations. More woodland habitat
is in the raccoon's interest. What's in the interest
of that wren calling, or the moss mat beneath my hand,

the vine maple, or the genes in a snail,
or owl-shadowed wings now crossing
the canyon wall, or the cockleburs anchored
to my boot lace?

Landscapes on Opening Night

The Dryopteris[1] is disappointed
in the artists' renditions:

The ferns resemble no offspring
of the present, the Permian,
the Jurassic, the Paleocene…

Those artists are perhaps myopic
or possibly, they've added
too much mycorrhiza to their tea.

The Dryopteris asks her maid,
"Am I being planthropomorphic?"
The maid bows as if a fiddlehead,

"It's not my place to say."

Affection, Affliction of Nematodes

From my pack, I pull a hand towel,
feign to wipe a smudge from your face.

In the woods, you press against so many trees,
I think not too much upon the transparent worms

end-to-end, tenth of a tenth of an inch, reeling
through the field of fuzz, a portion of your love

roaming down your cheek. Nor of their notoriety
in firing wormy poop up to a meter down range

from their powerful anal cannons. Your affection
will soon end, not for the trees, not for the 'todes,

but for me. Yet tonight, our mouths will ebb and roll
among consummate dipthong and vowel.

Tongues push, rise and fall in atonal song.

Polemic in Fragments

You and I have courted, even clung
to the run of the *'isms*, to the essences
of numerous *'ologies* and sacred canons.

Still have a calling? No, you are not chosen; none
under the sun are chosen—none. The Great Chain
didn't; the Great Chain of Being   isn't.

Three writers—writers of scripture
stumble into a bar,
stumble into one another.

"It's a miracle!" cries one.
"Embarrassing," mutters the second.
"Gin and tonic," says the third.

Like them, I'm with you for a round, and two
or three run-on sentences. If you must concoct
a rebuttal, please nest it in a country western song,

sprinkle in *God's Special Plan, no. 955 or 599;*
For God so loved the squirrels, no, the shales; don't
form a line; it's to no avail, God

is a geologist (it all makes sense now), perpetually
preoccupied with rock, or is all His time being spent
(and I'm speculating here) on Olympic marmots?

Between
the
Minutiae

Breeze
narrows,   unfurls
amid
moss
branches,
weighed   not by
those
who
sprint
over   the
stands-
zas.

Thrusting chicken heads

meter the lines, each ending
in punctuated peckwilibrium,
and stanzas finalized as grit
arrive in the gizzard quarry.

With your arm extended, stop
this story, block this image.
Recall the mist engulfing
a castle's crumbling walls.

The moat, now matures
as wetland. Treasure within—
what's precious without.
Mating calls of frogs pause.

Now, back to the chickens…

THERE

Bits of Green Lake, Northeast Seattle

A crow family across from Orin Court turns over Norway maple leaves.

It's too soon yet for someone to sweep the bald cypress needles; i.e.,
sweep them off the roof of the groundskeeper's shack. On the path,

the yellows decompose into a burnished golden mash. The mowers
turn up most days, grinding up oak and maple leaves into fine, bran-sized flakes.

The squirrels (eastern grays) walk up, look you in the eye,
then return to the bases of golden rain trees.

Two- and five-needled pines turn the lawns along Aurora nearly brown.
Will the Parks people vacuum them up, or ask the fungi to break them down?

At the south end, clouds thin, the sun thickens, the mirror of the lake
starts/finishes/vanishes a few hundred yards north of where this human is
standing.

Birches shed their leaves onto the green grass (gold coins);
cottonwoods continue to hoard theirs. Dogs are out

walking their masters, a white cockerpoo stands knee-deep in the lake;
a human on shore shouts at her in machine-like intervals.

28

I miss

the black-chinned hummingbirds,
a species thought to have perhaps
soared among the vine maple here

and the interrupted space
that their offspring would
now ripple and displace.

I miss the unscripted movements
of the chipping sparrows hunting along
maianthemum[2] and twin flower runs.

I miss the star sedge once residing
at Newman Lake and the insects
relying on it and *Acorus americanus* [3]

more or less, more of us;
less of everything else,
"moraless." I miss

salamanders gone, their log tenements
extracted, overcome by lawn
and single-family houses,

the leopard frogs leaping, loving along
the Walla Walla and Pend Oreille;
I miss the bobcats,

the invertebrates never born, the vegetation
they lived on, overwhelmed by English laurel,
English ivy, English holly, English.

I miss the murrelets that once flew here
before the old growth was cut down.
Even the big logs are gone

and the pinned-up hair of canopy cover,
and much of the wavy cotton moss,
and the lettuce lichens,

and squirrels with wings. Enable them
(or one of yours) to root or roost
outside the kitchen window,

and add your emptiness to mine.

Yao Han Center, Richmond, BC

Golden Rice Bowl
      Chun Hing   Wah Yuen   Seoul Express
                                    Curry House

Before the parking lot fills,
the noodle house gate is up.
Customers and coats are bundled
on chairs, upright plastic grocery bags
flaming up from the food court tables.

Chairs scrape in long single syllables,
chopsticks speak more softly in noodle bowls.
I see baseball caps, coffee and tea,
all the fast-food places lit in red or green.

A lady rubs cream onto her hands.
Old fellows break from conversation,
engage both sticks and spoon,
corral their noodles.

Unshaven Caucasian stands—
a statue off to one side
on the fringe. Eyes fixed.

Nisqually Refuge Tanka

Elderberries edge the delta's levee—
fluid limbs atop coarse trunks
standing
on warted bark of others;
my onus also.

Bicycling the Bicentennial Shelterbelt Trail, 2089
For A. Kokott

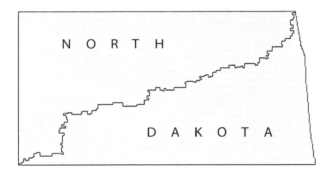

We start after the first hard-killing frost, the bees
curled up for the winter, most insects in a stupor.
We pedal down unending rows of juniper, cedar.
Zigzag north, east, occasionally retreat, a trail of
line segments, joined by convenient right angles
fashioned by farmers, ranchers, tribes, scientists.

Shadows wither, weaken; we roll through them.
We bed down at a B & B, then cross the Missouri,
pass through green ash, plums, willows and lilacs,
bike past an outhouse signed, *Hudson Bay Divide*,
      tune with the horn of the Burlington Northern,
      angle northeast toward Canada, the Red River.

      Farmers grumble, *Oh, those trees will invite rusts,*
      the down branches, late melting snowdrifts, trees,
      they're in the way of crossing from point B to point A.
      Nonetheless, farmers sign up for the state set-aside,
      but pole saws ride on tractors and, like barber poles,
      urge on some trimming, loppers too, alert in overalls.

The Bicentennial Shelterbelt Trail, January, 2090

        park behind the south-facing snowy cars
ski through lanes of willows green ash yarrow pods   the blizzard

       stop at the sign saying
          pheasant rest area somewhat
chip the snow crust from the park bench

remember mother once said that *she* was a known quantity

         wind layers
                    sifts the white bits
                       do crystals tinge the sound
          air blows past them
horizon to horizon gray glaze of lead pencil white in between you are not
entirely sure
       rather you are entirely not sure that you hear properly when the air is
nearly zero and the wind chilly
as well as noisy perhaps utterly and yet not so much entirely

  wait to see if any skier comes by   adverbs
                   in ridges
             drift   behind the trees

The Bicentennial Shelterbelt Trail, Spring, 2091

Never mind what Sally said, she'll pick us up
near Edinburg, though we break up,
are broken, will be broken, she'll pick us up.

The trail steers us toward dust storming—
no longer unusual in May, it billows from a harrow.
Choke now, or wait 'til the tractor plods to the end of the field.

Past the field's stone pile, the poem moves to a new place;
the shelterbelt dwindles, runs downhill, becomes
a tractor track loosely fitted with oak, willow, sumac. They

unlike us cannot descend out of the wind, the ground
has been allowed to grow its grass borders, but muscling in
are small rosettes of dandelion, shepherd's purse and prairie onion,
also bits of columbine, a bank of buttercup, hidden primrose,
and the remains of four or five white violets.

I wish I was armed with an excuse to stop here,
nor will you want to sit on the bank at the river.
Sally will meet us in Edinburg. I hope that
she is satisfied with what's happening here.

**Longmire Meadows;
Trail of the Shadows**

We rest on a bench wedded to the travertine.
A half-moon silhouettes the distant Douglas fir
and clouds chiffon the light over Longmire.
A bat cyclones past your curls and cattail.
Behind our bench, tired cedar tiptoe to the marsh:

Recline your head for an hour,
thoughts fall softly away. Electrons
once excited now nap in the leaves.
The stigma of unanswered anthers, the faint
aroma of unrequited wintergreen bells,

even pipsissewa and protozoa pause.
In the darkness you sigh to silence,
resting your head for an hour.
Your hair tumbles, tickles my lips;
You twist your torso in the darkness.

An owl instills a vowel into the seams
of the frogs' discourse. My nose
plays with the pine-lichened air,
the scent of drying moss. Momentarily,
I forget about the chocolate in your pocket.

A nick (Lakota Poem)

A little gray bird in a blast of wind
arrives from west beyond the Big Horns.
Mindful of tradition, yet to the sewing bag
pushing to add, enlarging.
She kindles a fire at noon
among the soft new snow.

Wo·ȟci

Zi·tka·la ci·k'a·la ȟo·te ta·te·yaŋ·p̓a ma·he
wi·yo·ȟpe·ya·taŋ-haŋ Ḣeš·ka a·ko·taŋ·haŋ hi ya ye.
Wó·o·pe wa·a·wa·ciŋ, ška paŋ·wo·tu·ka el
i·gla·ye·ǩi·ya yu·taŋ·ǩa·ya.
Wí·co·ǩaŋ·yaŋ ék·ta
wa·hi·šna·he·ca e´·gna yu·í·le.

Pronunciation key: a (father); c (chair); e (pet); h (hat); ȟ (gutteralized); i (wiener); k (kit); ǩ (go); k´ (glottal stop); n (nose); ŋ (bungalow); i (machine); o (oak); p (pink); p̓ (be); s (say); š (show); t (take); t̓ (doe); u (boot); w (way); y (yes); z (zero). The second syllable of words is accented unless indicated otherwise. Note: All adjacent vowels are pronounced separately.

Wohci

Zitkala cikala hote tateyanpa mahe
wiyohpeyatan-han Heska akotanhan hiyaye.
Woope waawacin, ska panwotuka el
iglayekiya yutankaya.
Wicokanyan ekta
wahisnaheca egna yuile.

Your Task List at a Limestone
Road Cut East of Emporia
on Old Highway 50

1. Park on the shoulder, lay asters on the rocks,
pay your respects to the remains of sea life
transformed into calcium carbonate blocks
bedded here in goldenrod, rough-leaf and sumac.

2. Cheer on the ants climbing a rock face formed
at a time when our sun cruised higher overhead,
sun blazing hot on what was then a shallow sea.
Seek shade in the nearby giant horsetail swamps.

3. Pick up an ice cube-sized chunk of limestone,
about 100 grams, around three and a half ounces:

> "100," coincidentally, the sum of the atomic weight
> of the atoms in a molecule of calcium carbonate
>
> so that the number of these $CaCO_3$ molecules
> will approximate Avogadro's number: 6.02×10^{23},
>
> or think of it as six hundred two billion
> and then tack on twelve more zeros.

Imagine a case where every molecule in this chunk
of rock is itself the size of an ice cube:

4. Shape the cubes into a solid cylinder covering Kansas
and beyond—the edges nudging South Bend, Indiana;
Waco, Texas; Grand Forks, North Dakota and Montrose,
Colorado. The cubes begin to run out as the tower rises

to eleven or twelve thousand miles, the earth resembling
a planetary Tootsie Roll Pop. Impurities of aluminum,
iron, magnesium, and silicon are in sufficient quantities
to form a thin earth wrapper to cover your secret snack.

5. After you conclude construction, return to this quiet place.
Disassemble and discard the rocks responsibly.

Reifel Bird Sanctuary

Into the bird sanctuary midday,
midweek, midsummer where
the alders shape themselves into oaks
and the lanes are contoured
to the eye of Homo sapiens, and
suffice as work areas for towhees
and dragonflies. The breeze blows

continuous melancholy, blows
through the notes of the song sparrow,
through the croaks of the sandhill cranes.
My lips rest on the epidermis
of a ginger cookie. I walk along the lane,
a gallery membered by numerous spirits
some seen and only poorly understood.

Walking the Log over Maple Creek

We arrive from opposite ends
midpoint on
the hewn log bridge.
We match up well as the shorelines that sent us.

"Sitka willows," you say, pointing over my shoulder.
Your arm and finger wobble
like a compass
arrow.

Stems faintly arched, leaf coat a singular green.
Beneath them, the creek riffles,
sun-capped, silkened stones
crumpling the water's vowels.

Your torso twists at the note
of a wayward thrush.
Vanilla leaf whiffs beneath
the uncertain sway of mountain alder.

Buck Lake Manuscripts

Inspired by After the Ice Age
by E.C. Pielou

Northeast of Mount Rainier,
a shallow lake bottom battles
decomposition. Carcasses
of algae, black alpine sedge,
huckleberry leaves all drift

downward through cemeterial waters,
joining the bones of tadpoles, mollusks,
and sepals from strawberries running
on shore, and great numbers of pollen
from spruce, from noble and subalpine fir.

On shore, my two companions are wrapped
to a log, gathering sun like lethargic iguanas.
Blue darner dragonflies hector the air
over a shoreline dimpled by bird tracks,
deer tracks, my tracks.

Spiders launch their web strings
and arc in breezes over the lake.
Beneath the water the annual layer
thickens. A thimble of muck
contains a thousand pollen grains.

Thirty linear feet of lake bottom contains
muck in nine thousand annual layers.
Someone's job is to identify the remains,
assemble a notion of what lived
and died here through time. Note:

In examining the evidence
a species' presence or absence,
retreat or invasion
were not predetermined
for my gratification.

The Douglas Minnesota Trail
on the Summer Solstice

I assume that you and I will be listening to the evening, listening.
    We step around a flattened mole. Here, at the trailhead,
two moms with SUV-like strollers encourage us to get moving.

Westward, through the cottonwood gaps are gabled roofs,
    the signage, "Pine Island Cheese," the Legion,
the memorial, the howitzer. The view is abruptly disrupted by a cabbage butterfly.

Ten feet away, the white butterfly turns, reverses, dips. "Unpredictable," you say,
    "as the trajectories of bombs and nerve gas in June of 1988." You carry
the Iran-Iraq war around like a bloody surgical sponge. And you go on:

"Wind tide rolls. The riverbank pollen goes airborne: surface-to-surface missiles.
    None of the villagers argued with Omar when he said his son died in vain.
Easier to comfort him: "Oh, he's in heaven now.'"

We go on for about a mile or two. Some companions of mine would have
    debated about shutter speeds, or their mother-in-law's kitchen cupboards,
recited Browning, mumbled a Hail Mary, or crowed about some restaurant.

Three doves roost tightly on a box elder branch above us. About-face,
    we walk north-northwest, the sun, low, dangles just left of our path ahead,
shining on this thick green lung of trail rising above the cornfields and cattle.

Tomorrow, I'll rise a few blocks from here. Will you have buried that war?
    I'll keep in mind your assertion: In Basrah and Mehran, voices call.
Something is needed over there other than a path winding past a memorial.

Mid-March Thaw on the Road to Longmire

The sun shouts from clouds so rarely tealed.
It wrings from the road a helical trail of spray.
Spattering water and sunlight grip the windshield.

Snow dollops on the topside of branches yield
the fluff plummeting onto my Chevrolet.
The sun sprouts from clouds so rarely tealed.

The fate of the road snow is inexorably sealed.
Limbs spring upward, their burdens fall away
spattering water. And sunlight grips the windshield.

Rounding a curve, old-growth darkness concealed
yet unconcealed where the Kautz and Nisqually rivers mate.
The sun pokes out from cloud bundles tealed.

High up, the mountain rock holds fast in the white Bastille.
The odd cloud coloring will last less than a day.
Vagabond water and sunlight grip the windshield.

The sun's worn off the melancholy, your radiance revealed.
I pray that the calm elation in the car might stay.
The sun's ablaze in clouds so rarely tealed,
Crab Nebula spatter (organic matter) grips the windshield.

S

H

O

R

T

S

On Steens Mountain

Flowers flinching atop
      swaying stems—coyote mint
in shifting winds.

      Butterflies in their checkered spots
and sweat bees striped in black and white
      ride the flowered canopy—

winged cowboys
      whose mounts abide
but one rider at a time.

Sitting

       on the curb,
softly chanting a roll call
       of seed pods,
rudely interrupted when
an outspoken weed nods.

Ars Poetica

Periods when the blood
refuses to run,
I become a casket
on a church truck,
circling inside a nameless plaza.
Unpredictable horn blasts,
satin sweats against my skin.

Urban Park

No human sounds late at night.
Loose dogs and cats on the chase
inspire stress in all vertebrates.

Family pets spend their strength
then nap in the pickup
as master heads for home.

Rabbit found dead next morning,
run into the ground, exhausted,
died from not being caught.

Insect Crucifixion

I was born a rather common
19th century British beetle—
one of Darwin's darlings.

Pinned through
my right
 wing
cover

    ,

purchase me for 8 farthings.

Crows on Campus

peer through the library windows,
they've undergone much scrutiny,
enjoy a degree of security,
appear nearly content—

a bit like humans lined up
at the cash register, groceries
fresh for the night's meal, tabloids
not quite mirrored in their faces.

Pheasants[5]

forage in a Dutch wetland
rolling moss balls out of Dicranum
and Mnium moss mats.
A bit like knitting in reverse.

Wilbur from Kwantung Province
For Robert Hayden

"Weebo," they called him,
anyone 'round town anyways.
Everyone knew Weebo.
He was okay.

Nights when we play rummy,
his discard would get picked
and he'd frown and say "Gog Dong."
He knew it right, but

Gog Dong had served and saved him
through the twenties, thirties, forties.
That and the wife and later,
his Ronald Reagan haircut.

GROWING

CURIOUS

ABOUT

HUMANS

Henry Satulick[6]

Your shoes meld a soft tempo to
Doppler drones of insects winged.
This veined percussion fades,
you look back to the mountain
and September's aging meadow.

Among the waves of green heather are
the buff of abandoned oat grass glumes,
golden leaves of western pasque flower,
the unruly white cotton of undergreen willow
and the fuzz of olive green lupine pods.

Always your gaze, I cannot measure.
Your forehead squints into crevices of
unwalkable ledges, unreadable signs.
I await the comfort of your campfire when
you recount to me images I do not fathom.

I drink from my water, walk through a prayer:
Spirit meadow, call the elk to your waters.
After the hunt, bring clouds low to your care,
healing, hiding mothers, young sons and daughters.
And allow us to walk among the sedges for a time.

Stone Ruin on Old Man Burman's Lawn

Across the road, he mows ahead of the rain
    and as in past years, he reaches the lawn's
center where he circles around the statuary—
    a pagoda missing its head. What's left
stands as a three-foot pillar listing
    ten degrees from the perpendicular.

When he mows next to it, I say to myself,
    "This time, he'll decide something needs to be done."
But the pagoda continues to lean, remains topless.
    What flows through the heads of the kids (now adults)
who stole it—when they drive by—when they repeatedly
    note the roof's absence now after twenty summers?

Saturday: the rain again threatens. The grass
    needs cutting, Burman and I are mowing.
I wonder why humans are obsessed with sharp corners,
    definite borders, but I equally marvel at Burman's ability
to cast the image of the pagoda aside while neighbors
    squint and shrug at his unended sentence.

I unplug my mower. Across the street on the pagoda's pillar
    stands a California quail; a little black plume on his forehead
jounces as this sentinel surveys the road and yard.
    That quail's shade of blue like lilac but a tad more gray—
like old man Burman's overalls there in the front bay window.
    Burman, are you determined not to roof your pagoda?

Try

to recall that promising summertime party:
Ladies in their fifties in broad-brimmed hats,
the muscular man in the Indian suit, circling
work tables membered by caterers stirring
chicken salads swirled in thick Pyrex bowls.

2.

And the rotisserie of pig, endlessly dripping,
mesmerizing the pipes attached to grimaces
of men in polo shirts, a golden retriever whose
remarkable name I cannot quite recollect. He
circles the pit, settles on the patio's fringe.

3.

Men in the garage pose a preparatory stance,
working up admiration for the model railroad cars
now bridging a paper river, now circling, cycling.
The host holds a shoebox of miniature people; he
punctuates essential points over the engine din.

4.

Are you sorry that we could not quite hear him?
Someone turns aside, mutters, *No ambulance.*
His friend: *Before Lionel, it was matchbooks?*
Yes, and before… The train lurches. *continuity…*
stereo steel squealing. Guests move doorward.

5.

Night falls, pockets of laughter; floating, red burning
Marlboros belaying marked conversation. Lone dog
whines in the kitchen. Patio door slides eastward,
reverses direction. Semi-secret lovers remain lost,
not hidden in the rhododendron and cotoneaster.

6.

No, you remember a different party, but wait:
the garage, mixing bowls, a clacking of heels
on the patio planks... My hearing is so poor,
unknown to me until now, it has venomized
my description. Repair it with your recollection.

Observations

In May, you stopped leaving notes.
In July, the phone lies prone—
seems as though you've squeezed
a thousand acquaintances
through ever narrower sieves.

Now you remain every day
next to Ray drawing pictures of snails
in apartment three. Or when it rains
or snows, you're out-of-doors
consorting with crows, sparrows, squirrels.

If I mention that your life is without balance
you reply that I harbor a distant malice
not supportive, hardly a partner. I'm so removed
from the dirt, from the humus. You hiss
if I suggest a vacation to Vegas.

Your life is scaled to a different balance.
Ears turn red when Uncle Johnson says
 "Leave it up to the good Lord."
You are a limp, waterlogged paper towel, incapable
of holding even one drop of adversity.

You mumble in concert with each utterance
of every woman, of every man.
"Out of the mouths of Homo sapiens."
And at night, when I turn off the light,
your tears flow without apparent prologue.

Parting Sparks

When I no longer am able to think or walk,
wheel me out to the ravine in the forest—
make it November, when leaves of cottonwood
abscise downward insisting on soft, fussy collisions,
falling on sword ferns and moss.

Receptors in my eyes may still hold on to an image
of the fine wiring of daintily branched cicely plants,
their skeletons still standing, now more than meek
below red huckleberry arms that perpetually wave
above hard-fought-for stumps.

You must see for me the weathered maple leaves
dangling like families of bats from clustered branches
and the midafternoon sun dispersing the fog, inviting
the lemony cottonwood leaves to join me and the gold
slowly decaying on the decomposing mat.

Snippets Seen from the Kitchen Window

"I do love yard work," you proclaim
before slinging the hoe, slamming it
against the far garden wall. Quickly, you
turn your attention to pulling, pulling

the lawn mower cord. When did your nose
start bleeding? You saw at the grass—
little half-assed cuts, your tight little smile
engulfed in blue smoke   —A-R-G-H-R-R—

Why are you now flat on your stomach
in the ditch? An empty glove propels the mower
toward the house. Its journey ends with paint
and sparks barking from the rain spout.

You reglove, draw your loppers, and turn
to the blackberry. Wouldn't you like to break
for a beer? You lop one cane again
and again. What's left is a mere pencil stub.

But this piece must be punished—you fit
it lengthwise between the lopper blades… Oh no,
you catch your pinkie between the handles.
You dance and scream like a wounded weasel.

A someone somewhat familiar
trudges up to the kitchen door.
Your nose in just twenty-four lines
is now the purple of a ripe Bing cherry.

Memorial Service

My pen scores
the speaker's
every phrase.
In the pause
between eulogies
a woman
I do not recognize
hands to me
a slip of paper,
size of a holy card
then caps her pen
as the drone from
the dais begins again.

Elsewhere on stage
flowers lie: some
draped over the casket's
poplar vest. Others
lie high on black, wired
scaffoldings—surrogates
for squadron campfires
lining the beach
our vessels
loathed to reach.
Destine no flower
at my end
for me.

Minnesota Centennial

The flatbed smoothly ebbs
down Central Avenue.
Pet Parade, 1958.

Because I have freckles
I have been anointed, painted
in brown, gold, black stripes.

I pose as a small mammal
on a bed of papier-mâché green grass.
Sign on the float says

We offer the Gopher another hundred years.

In November of 1961,
I glob onto guys walking
along expansive weathered lawns.

The one in charge carries
gunnysacks. To this gang
I aspire to be a member.

Others carry one-gallon water jugs.
One yells, points at a small brown blur
that disappears among the grass blades.

They rush forward, discover and flood
the tiny gopher holes. Others, holding sacks,
bag gophers leaping from their homes.

I walk with no one in particular as
the group walks over to the river,
onto the walkway over the dam.

They upend their bags, dumping the rodents
into the deep. Most begin paddling;
they try to climb onto the concrete ledge.

The boys poke them with sticks
and press them under until all are drowned—
seems like five minutes.

What gang do I aspire to now?

SOMETHING
HOLY
IN
SCIENCE

Mole Calling
For Marlene Zuk, Biologist

A mole lies on a Redmond trail
extra large, totally intact, deceased.

Did she ascend from the ground
seeking some open-air freedom?

Perhaps like pill bugs, she harbors
worms in her stomach that sense

that the end is near, so like sirens
they summon their host to the surface

for their own purpose.

Carolina's Road

beneath
my bicycle
winds,
linearly folds,
squeezes
t
h
r
o
u
g
h
pine,
red maple.

Brakes
end
the
ticks
the popping
beneath my tires.

My pen waddles with the wind,
words labeling the workings of tiny things
I cannot understand nor see; wind shuffles
the leaves—epidermis—protein synthesis,
molecules in cells colliding
thousands
of times
per
second.

Ride, numbskull.

Rubber spins
  against
    the grit.
  I remain
     fixed
     in the cells,
      pedals
    submerged
  in cytoplasm,
    wheeling
     past folding
     proteins, squeezing
      past
       ribosomes.

For Alan Smith

SOMETHING
ELSE

Sketchily Measuring the Predicaments
in Increments in the Adverb Castle District

Nearing the moat, she rallies, staggering arhythmically
through oaks and vines. Being nearly of separate minds,
she clumsily four-syllables through the last of the timber.
She has filled her bag with adverbs from across the land
plus a smattering of adjectives to preserve bland freshness.
She seeks sanctuary in adverb castle and as she draws near,
a voice calls out, "We're quite sure that no one is here."

A carriage pulls up behind her. In it sits eminently His Eminence,
marginally rotunder than his associates, significantly *profounder*
in matters of faith, morals and consequently incontinence (p < .001).
Had Chaucer been invited, they would have perhaps stopped
in the piss-poor manor, since the prioress known as Fervant Lee
stoically reads all pilgrim poetry. In conversation, she's a name-dropper
or self-righteous or judgmental 86 percent of the time, approximately.

Musical notes frequently fly merrily from the castle: the horns
pierce the sky mightily, the oboe whines in the ear despondently.
The conductor, celloist and fiddler paddle behind stage, the six beats
per measure are consistently coherent if you nod off from time to time—
the castle walls notwithstanding. The woman who reached the moat
heralds those not quite present within the walls: *Roughly half of us*
engage periods periodically—not for punctuation, not quasi-consciously.

Litany of the Plants[7]

Cantor: **Assembly:**

Sun, remain constant,   Sun, remain constant,
In radiance,   Sun, remain constant,
Earth, remain constant,   Earth, remain constant,
In orbit,   Earth, remain constant,
Embrace the ancients—   Earth, remain constant,
Those alive,   Embrace the ancients,
Their remains,   Embrace the ancients,
Their descendants   Earth, remain constant,
The plants' mycorrhizal comrades,   Earth, remain constant

Oceans, remain constant,   Oceans, remain constant,
Oceans, recycle your life forms,   May you maintain and flourish,
Clouds, come forth,   May you maintain and flourish,
Release your waters,   May you maintain and flourish,
That the air remains healthy,   May it maintain and flourish,
That elements remain in balance.   That the air remains healthy.

Sun, shine on,   Sun, remain constant,
Smile on green algae,   Sun, remain constant,
Smile on the blue-greens,   Sun, remain constant,
Smile on the hornworts,   Sun, remain constant,
Smile on the liverworts,   Sun, remain constant,
Smile on the mosses,   Sun, remain constant,
Smile on the club mosses,   Sun, remain constant,
Smile on the ferns,   Sun, remain constant,
Smile on the conifers,   Sun, remain constant,
Smile on the flowering plants,   Sun, remain constant.

Litany of the Plants

Dux:

Sol, mane fidelis,
In candelabra,
Terra, mane fidelis,
In orbis,
Amplectere prokarya—
Haec viva
Reliquias suas,
Et eukarya,
Fungi-sodales plantarum,

Oceani, manete fidelis,
Oceani, dissolvite animas suas,
Nubes venite,
Liberate aquas suas,
Ut caelum salvum conservet,
Ut atomi maneat in proportionem.

Sol, luceat in diuturnitatem,
Adfulge super Chlorophyta,
Adfulge super Cyanobacteria,
Adfulge super Anthocerotophyta,
Adfulge super Marchantiophyta,
Adfulge super Bryophyta.
Adfulge super Lycopodiacis,
Adfulge super Polypodiacis,
Adfulge super Pinacis,
Adfulge super Angiosperma,

Conventus:

Sol, mane fidelis,
Sol, mane fidelis,
Terra, mane fidelis,
Terra, mane fidelis,
Terra, mane fidelis,
Amplectere prokarya,
Amplectere prokarya,
Terra, mane fidelis,
Terra, mane fidelis

Oceani, manete fidelis,
Sustineatis et floreatis,
Sustineatis et floreatis,
Sustineatis et floreatis,
Sustineat et floreat,
Ut caelum salvum conservet.

Sol, mane fidelis,
Sol, mane fidelis,
Sol, mane fidelis,
Sol, mane fidelis,
Sol, mane fidelis,
Sol, mane fidelis,
Sol, mane fidelis,
Sol, mane fidelis,
Sol, mane fidelis,
Sol, mane fidelis.

Litany of the Plants (continued)

Cantor: **Assembly:**

Cantor:	Assembly:
From all evil, deliver the plants,	Earth, deliver the plants,
From nitrogen excess,	Earth, deliver the plants,
From nuclear accident,	Earth, deliver the plants,
From genetic engineering,	Earth, deliver the plants,
From human negligence,	Earth, deliver the plants,
From human indifference,	Earth, deliver the plants,
From human vanity,	Earth, deliver the plants,
From human greed,	Earth, deliver the plants,
From all human excesses,	Earth, deliver the plants,
From drought,	Earth, deliver the plants,
From disease,	Earth, deliver the plants,
Plants, deliver us,	Plants, deliver us,
Through thy fruits,	Plants, deliver us,
Through thy shelter,	Plants, deliver us,
Through thy steadfastness,	Plants, deliver us,
Through thy tranquility,	Plants, deliver us.

Let us pray: It is perhaps not within you to grant atonement for injustices, but let the wealth in your continued existence reflect the dissolution of our injustices. Amen.

Litany of the Plants

Dux:	**Conventus:**
Ab omni malo, terra, libera plantas,	Terra, libera plantas,
Ab fluvia nitrogenumi,	Terra, libera plantas,
Ab fluvia radiatione,	Terra, libera plantas,
Ab pericula genetica,	Terra, libera plantas,
Ab incuria humana,	Terra, libera plantas,
Ab lentitudine humana,	Terra, libera plantas,
Ab vanitate humana,	Terra, libera plantas,
Ab avaritia humana,	Terra, libera plantas,
Ab omni immoderatione humana,	Terra, libera plantas,
Ab siccitate,	Terra, libera plantas,
Ab morbo,	Terra, libera plantas,
Libera nos, plantae,	Libera nos, plantae,
Per fruges tuas,	Libera nos, plantae,
Per perfugium tuum,	Libera nos, plantae,
Per stabilitatem tuam,	Libera nos, plantae,
Per animam tranquillam,	Libera nos, plantae.

Oremus: Fortisan non possitis concedere veniam
pro delictis, sub divitiae suae et vita dissipationem
delictarum nostarum monstrant. Amen.

82

Notes

[1]Landscapes on Opening Night: Dryopteris is a large genus of ferns found in Asia, the Americas, and Oceania. The main character in the poem is thought to be a member of *Dryopteris expansa*, the spiny wood fern.

[2]I Miss: *Maeanthemum dilatatum*: Common name is "false lily of the valley."

[3]*Acorus Americanus*: Common name is "American sweet flag," a wetland plant growing in Canada and the northern U.S.

[4]The poet recognizes the research and observations of several individuals, including: Curtis R. Bjork, Ronald C. Friesz, William R. Leonard, Kathy R. McAllister, Ed Newbold, and resources at the Burke Museum.

[5]Pheasants: Based on work by J. Wiegers reported in *Beitrage zur Biologie der Pflanzen* 58 (3):449-454.

[6]Henry Satulick: Known to white settlers as "Indian Henry." Also, "Suterlick" or "Soo-Too-Lick." A meadow and mountain are named for this Native American in the southwest portion of Mount Rainier National Park.

[7]Litany of the Plants: Format is loosely based on the "Litany of the Saints" from Dom Gaspar Lefebvre's *Saint Andrew Daily Missal*, published by E. M. Lohmann, St. Paul, Minnesota, 1937.